THE GRATITUDE

BEADS

Julie J. Tennis

Pocket Stone Press

Naselle, WA

While many elements in this story are real, the people are not. Any similarity to actual humans is coincidental.

Pocket Stone Press
P.O. Box 425
Naselle, Washington, 98638 USA

The Gratitude Beads / Julie J. Tennis. —1st ed.
ISBN 979-8-9854876-0-2 (print)
ISBN 979-8-9854876-1-9 (ePub)

Contents

For Mom, who nurtured my creativity from the beginning.

How It Began

Sarah stared at the screen of her laptop, suddenly aware of how long she'd been sitting with her finger on the mouse, scrolling through the same old memes and status updates that had been there yesterday, and the day before. A thought floated to the surface, *How did my life become so shriveled up and small?* Working from home had been wonderful, especially when her elderly dog, Peaches, was still alive, but now it just felt draining. She was exhausted, unmotivated, and felt guilty that she wasn't living the life she had imagined for herself.

I need to shake myself out of this, she thought. Sarah remembered how walks with Peaches used to help clear her mind. Picturing Peaches bounding around on the local logging roads motivated Sarah to close her laptop. She dragged her listless body out the door with hopes of working off the lethargy that seemed to permeate every cell. She took a right at the end of the driveway and headed for the forested hills that encircled the small town.

Halfway up the steep slope of the first hill, the logging road bent to the left and Sarah's gaze was filled with the glowing, mottled gray stems of alder trees, lit by the afternoon sun. Their uniform, straight trunks lifted her spirits; something about the play of light and the energy of the trees themselves gave her pause, distracting her mind from the long, uphill trudge.

As her gaze moved over the trees, a spot of red caught her eye. Curious, she walked closer, then turquoise, purple, green and white came into view. They were small glass beads tied along a thin black cord. The cord had snagged on a low branch a few feet into the forest, along a deer trail. It felt numinous, a little piece of colorful magic among the gray-stemmed trees.

Sarah looked around. That path led up to a bit of private property tucked into the commercial timberlands at the top of the hill. She remembered an old trailer parked back in there. Maybe these beads belonged to whomever lived in it. She pulled the cord off the branch and continued up the road. The beads caught the afternoon light and sparkled as Sarah drew them through her fingers.

Sarah gazed into the alder thicket at the top of the hill. She could see the dark shape of the trailer hidden in trees, about fifty feet from the logging road. The alders had really grown up since Peaches died. Sarah crossed her arms and absentmindedly toed the dirt. It was dark and eerily quiet inside the grove. She took a deep breath and headed in.

A tingly shiver of fear creased up Sarah's back as she reached out to knock on the mildew-covered door of the trailer. Under her thoughts were half-remembered news casts and Grimm's fairy tales, warning her of the danger of isolated homes in dark forests. Her anxiety grew as her knuckles rapped a second time on the door.

As she reached to hang the beaded cord on the doorknob, a voice behind her said, "Can I help you?"

Sarah yelped and turned, falling against the trailer. The door handle pressed into her back as the metal step scraped her bare calf.

A woman stood several feet away, a broad basket hanging off her arm. Her graying hair was pulled back in a loose bun, a few wisps floating free around her kind face. She looked to be in her 60's. The basket flowed over with a variety of leaves and flowers.

Sarah clutched at her heart, "You scared me!"

"I can see that. My apologies," said the woman. "Is there a reason you've come knocking at my door?"

Sarah took a deep breath. "Yes, I found this hung up on a branch down the hill and thought it might be yours." Sarah held up the string of bright glass beads.

The woman's features softened, and her mouth curved into a wide smile. It was the kind of smile Sarah used to see on her grandmother's face, a smile of pure loving acceptance. The woman asked, "Would you like to come in?"

Sarah paused for a moment, then said, "Sure." All thoughts of danger evaporated in the kind energy coming from the woman. *This is just someone's grandma living off the land*, she thought. Then she followed the woman inside.

It took a moment for Sarah's eyes to adjust. She was expecting to be hunched over in the dark, cramped space of a trailer, but after passing through the door the area opened into a high-ceilinged room bright with sunlight. They had walked into a large yurt! The far wall was four or five paces away. The bamboo floor glowed like honey from the light coming in through the domed skylight high above. Curved walls were interspersed with windows and shelves containing books and artwork. A little nook contained drying racks, full of herbs.

Sarah stood in the entryway; her jaw dropping as she took in the huge room. She shook her head and went back outside. She put her hands on the outside of the small trailer. She could feel the gritty texture of the mildewy plastic. She walked around the perimeter, touching all the walls as if searching for hidden panels. The woman leaned out the door and asked, "Would you like some tea?" Sarah mumbled "yes" as she finished her circumnavigation and followed the woman back inside.

The woman gestured to a pair of overstuffed chairs next to a small table in the center of the room. Sarah took a seat, her head still swiveling as she tried to make sense of this unexpected space. "How is this possible," she asked.

"What's that?" the woman said.

"How is it that the inside of your trailer is an entirely different size and shape than the outside?"

"That's a great question," the woman replied, "but how about introductions first? My name is Voz."

"I'm Sarah."

"It's nice to meet you," Voz said, as she joined Sarah and set a tray with tea and scones on the low table between them. She poured Sarah, and then herself, a cup of fragrant tea. The woman lifted the plate of scones, offering, and Sarah took one.

"Thank you," she said, then took a bite. The crunchy outer layer gave way to a warm, fluffy interior; it was as if they had just been pulled from the oven. Sarah made an "mmm..." sound as she closed her eyes and chewed. "This is delicious!" she said.

Voz's face was relaxed as she sipped her tea, watching Sarah over the top of her cup. Sarah noticed Voz's eyes were deep green, like the needles of the Douglas fir trees on the other side of the logging road.

"Are you a witch?" Sarah asked.

Voz's head tilted back as she let out a bray of laughter. "Ha ha ha! No, I'm no witch."

"Then what are you," Sarah asked. "And why does this," she gestured her hands around the room, "look like a trailer on the outside and inside it is a spacious yurt?"

"Let's just say it's magic," Voz said. "Like that cord you found." Voz extended her palm. Sarah lifted the beaded cord from the table and handed it to the woman.

"These are gratitude beads," Voz said, running the beads through her fingers.

"I haven't heard of gratitude beads," Sarah said. "What are they?"

"They're a meditation tool," replied Voz, "meant to be used when walking out in nature. As you hold each bead, you bring to mind all the things in that element or area of your life for which you are grateful. You let them fill your heart, really *experiencing* the gratitude that you have for each thing."

"What do the beads represent?" Sarah asked.

"There are eight Nature beads and seven Self beads. The Nature beads help you to focus on the elements outside of yourself that make up the world you live in, and the Self beads help you focus on the seven foundational elements of your personal life," Voz said.

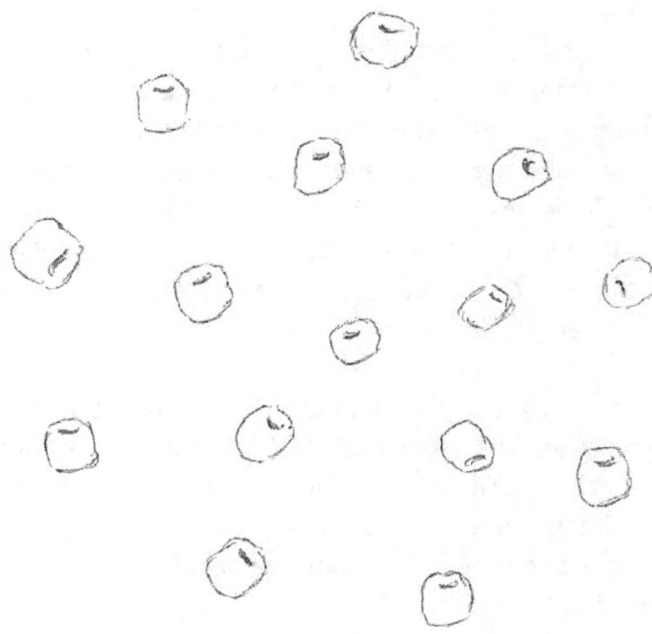

S arah leaned in as Voz gestured to the first bead after the knot. The bead was brown. Voz held it between her finger and thumb and said, "You start with the 'Earth' bead. As you walk, you hold the bead in your fingers and think about all that you are grateful for from the Earth."

As Voz spoke, the air between them began to shimmer and blur, like a halocline – the interface between salt and fresh water. She continued, "For example, I would say, 'I am grateful for Earth. I'm grateful for the rich soil and solid ground that feeds and supports the forests that surround us. I am grateful for the uplifted seafloor sediment that forms the hills where we live. And I'm grateful for the magnetic field of the planet that helps protect us from the solar winds.'"

As Voz described examples of what she was grateful for, shapes formed in the halocline and Sarah *saw* what Voz was describing. She *saw* the soil and hillside where they sat, *saw* how the clay layers of the ocean floor were scraped up against the continental shelf to form these hills; she even saw the entire planet, enveloped in its relatively thin atmosphere, so delicate, floating over the table as solar winds roared past.

Voz went on to describe examples for each of the beads as Sarah watched the changing images in the shimmering air between them. There were four elements, four directions with animals that Voz called "protectors," and seven different aspects of self – from the body to one's work in the world to the spirit.

After the last bead, Voz moved her fingers to the knot holding the string in a loop. "This knot," she said, "represents you, in this time and place. Each of us is a mix of elements that have been on Earth since its formation. The assemblage that makes up you, here and now, is unique. This knot reminds you to be grateful that you exist, and for all the other everyday miracles in your life. There is so much to be grateful for, yet we so easily fall into despair when things don't go our way. This knot also reminds you to give thanks for the unique problems that are yours to solve, and your ability to do so. If you were not here, imagine all that you have accomplished and will accomplish – undone. You may think you don't matter, but every little thing you've done and will do ripples out into the world, touching others in unseen ways."

Sarah saw herself in the shimmering air. She was walking in downtown Seattle. The image of herself glanced up with a big smile on her face as she passed a stranger. They made eye-contact. In the movie playing out before her, Sarah watched the stranger, a woman in her 40's, continue on her way to the Olive Way overpass. The woman gazed down on the speeding traffic of I-5. Sarah could imagine the woman's thoughts, as she has been there herself. Now she could *see* the woman's thoughts: the woman imagining herself climbing over the rail, hanging over traffic, and letting go. But then an image of Sarah's smiling face banished the dark thoughts. The woman paused, a soft smile on her own face; she stood taller, gazed back towards the city, and returned the way she had come.

Voz fell silent and the rippling air between them returned to normal.

Sarah's jaw hung open. She whispered, "wow." The idea that something as simple as a smile could alter someone's life so completely felt overwhelming, especially considering all the times she had looked up with a grimace on her face, agonizing over her own internal misery. How many people had she influenced into having a *bad* day?

She looked around for a distraction. The scone she'd taken a bite of earlier sat, forgotten, on the table. She picked it up and dipped it in her tea. Just as the submerged biscuit was about to crumble apart, Sarah lifted it to her mouth, following it with her cup. The sweet fragrance of jasmine floated up from the green tea, riding on a swirl of steam. The aroma and chewing helped to pull her back into her body, grounding her in the present moment. Sarah finished the scone and washed it down with the rest of her crumb-filled tea.

"Well," Voz said, breaking the long silence, "the best way to learn how to use the Gratitude Beads is to *use* them. Why don't you take them for a walk and see how it goes?"

Sarah set her cup on the table. "Okay," she said. "Would you like to come with me?"

"Gratitude Beads works best when you are alone with your thoughts," Voz replied.

Sarah stood and thanked Voz for the tea and the beads. As she headed out the door, she turned back and asked, "Can I visit you again?"

"Sure," Voz replied. "I'd like that!"

A few months later, during one of their daily visits, Sarah said to Voz, "I've noticed some days when I use the Gratitude Beads I feel as though I'm channeling the spirit of Life itself, as each gratitude fills my body and spills out into the world. Other days I feel like I'm just going through the motions, saying the words without any feeling or sense of connection."

Voz said, "It's normal for some days to feel more connected than others. I bet you've noticed that, even on those shriveled-up days, you feel a little better when you're done."

"It's true, I do," Sarah replied.

Voz's expression turned serious. "I have some news," she said.

Sarah's guts clenched at the change in Voz's demeanor. "What is it?"

"This property I've been parked on has been sold, and the new owner is going to be building a house here. It is time for me to move on."

Sarah's mind sped through different scenarios and emotions as she thought about losing her friend. "Where will you go," she asked. She paused for a moment, then said, "You can park in my driveway!"

"Thank you," said Voz, "but I'm actually looking forward to traveling for a while. There's still so much of the world that I want to see."

After Voz left Sarah found herself starting to slide back into the brain-numbing behaviors she'd been trying to escape so many months ago. Without her daily visits with Voz, her mind craved the imaginary friendships of social media and sitcomes. She spent more and more time with her computer. Thankfully, she was still going on her daily gratitude walks.

It was on one of these walks that Sarah realized that part of the reason she had felt so shriveled up before meeting Voz was because she was lonely. Perhaps she, too, needed a change of scenery.

She was holding the green bead of "relationships" in her fingers and pictured the faces of people she cared about living in the city. She'd originally moved down here for a job, and had stayed after it ended. Now she considered moving back, where there would be more opportunities to socialize, and she could be closer to her friends and family.

The following autumn, Sarah packed the rest of her things and headed north to Seattle. She was delighted to work in an office, with coworkers! And to have a long mid-day break that gave her time to take walks after lunch. The weather was starting to change, oscillating between bright warm days and rain. Today it was sunny outside. She still had time to catch some nice weather before the doldrums of a Pacific Northwest winter settled in.

Sarah stepped out on the sidewalk and gazed up at the strip of blue sky between the tall buildings. Inspired, she unwrapped the gratitude beads from her wrist. She let her feet guide her as she moved through the beads, pulling gratitudes from the world around her – that bit of soil in the planter where a tree grew, the bright sun reflecting off all the glass skyrises, a bird skittering down an alleyway, that stray cat.

She felt her face relax and her shoulders unwind after a morning of concentrated focus. Sarah felt light and expansive. A warm smile spread across her face. She glanced up as she passed a woman walking up Olive Way. They made eye-contact. Sarah smiled wider and said hello.

The Beads

This section contains descriptions for each of the 15 beads and provides example gratitudes for them. These are simply guidelines to help spark your own ideas and meanings for each bead, let inspiration and creativity guide you.

The colors in parentheses describe the beads that are available from the author. You can also make your own Gratitude Beads, with your own colors and descriptions. You can even use a piece of cord with knots in it, or no string at all. There is no way to do this wrong.

Earth (dark brown)
We begin here because Earth is the footing upon which Life exists. It is the landscapes that lift our hearts, the soil that grows our food, the gravity that holds us all in place. This element includes sand, silt, clay, and stone as well as bone, shell, and wood. We all have a bit of Earth inside of us. As you consider Earth, what gratitudes arise for you?

Air (clear)
Air connects us all together in breath, especially with our green siblings, the plants. It is the wind, the sky, and the atmosphere that encases our planet. It carries scent and sound and holds up the clouds. What are you grateful for from the element of Air?

Fire (red)
Fire is a gift from the Sun, who provides us with heat and warmth as well as light and all the colors we can see. The

fire of the Sun is stored in plants, where it can be drawn out to provide us light and warmth. Sun makes life possible by nourishing the plants, who feed us directly and indirectly, and who create oxygen for us to breath. What gratitudes does Fire conjure up for you?

Water (blue)
Water connects all Life; it flows through all things. It enables living things to move and grow. It is clouds, rain, and snow. It is puddles, ponds, lakes, creeks, streams and rivers. It permeates the soil and fills aquifers, makes wetlands, and gathers in the ocean. It covers most of our planet and makes up most of our bodies. What gratitudes do you have for Water?

Decades ago I took to referring to all living beings as people, to help break down the mental wall that places humans above all other forms of life. By thanking them for all they provide us, we are building our compassion towards other life forms and acknowledging the incredible debt we owe to them. The next four beads focus on our other-than-human relatives.

People of the West (turquoise)
The People of the West, Guardians of Water, are all those creatures and beings who inhabit the waters of the world. They are the aquatic invertebrates, fish, amphibians, and marine mammals. Their presence, or absence, tells us about the health of the water where they dwell. In this bead we embrace all the forms of life who fill the oceans, rivers, streams, ponds, pools, puddles and rivulets. Who do you appreciate who lives in water?

People of the North (gold)
The People of the North, Guardians of Earth, are all of those who live on or in lands around the world. They are

the invertebrates, reptiles, amphibians, birds and mammals who walk, slither, crawl and burrow in the earth. Who lives upon the land that makes your life better or more enjoyable?

People of the East (white)
The People of the East, Guardians of the Air, are all who are able to take flight or who call the sky their home. They are the invertebrates, birds and mammals who grace the skies with their flight and their songs. People of the sky tie worlds together. Who are you grateful for who has wings?

People of the South (olive green)
The People of the South, Guardians of Fire, are the beings who soak up and store the energy of the sun within their bodies. These are the trees, shrubs, forbs, mosses, algaes and lichens. They are the People of the Green. They provide us with food, medicine, clothing, dwellings, fire and oxygen. Without the People of the Green, we would not be able to exist. Which Guardians of Fire are you grateful for today?

Now that we have extended gratitudes to the elements and beings who support our ability to exist, we can bring our attention to all that is right in our own worlds, giving thanks to everything that gives us agency in our own lives.

Body (red)
Your body is the container that allows you to perceive and interact with the world. It is your senses, your muscles, your organs. Even if it doesn't look how you want it to or isn't as capable as you would like it to be, it is still giving you the opportunity to exist and interact with the world around you. What are you grateful for about your body?

Home (orange)
Your home is not just the dwelling where you sleep at night, it is also the neighborhood in which you dwell, the trails and roads you travel, the landscape on which you live, and the physical accoutrements of your life. When you look towards home, what gratitudes arise for you?

Work (yellow)
This bead represents your work in the world, including jobs you're paid to do, volunteer work, and passion projects you do on the side. This is your contribution to others, and how you make a living. Think about the benefits these bring to your life. What are you grateful for about your work?

Relationships (green)
Relationships include all the people with whom you regularly interact: your family, your friends, the animals you know, your colleagues, your neighbors. This includes those are no longer with you, and those who have yet to enter your life. Who are you grateful for today?

Self-Expression (blue)
Self-expression is your voice in the world, the part of yourself that you share with others. This includes how you speak, how you treat others, how you dress, and how you present yourself. It is what you stand for. It is also any of your creative endeavors you share with the world. The ability to express yourself is often taken for granted. What public aspects of yourself are you grateful for?

Mind (violet)
Your mind is your thinking self, your intellect. It includes your curiosity, your memory, and all that you have learned

over time. It is your ability to figure things out. What gratitudes do you have for your mental abilities?

Spirit (silver)

Spirit is your higher self, the part of you that connects with others at a soul level. It is your compassion, empathy and kindness. This is your connection to your higher power, to the existence beyond your existence, to the animating force, to the divine. It is the nudge that guides you in the right direction or into making right choices. What gratitudes does spirit conjure for you?

The Knot

The knot represents you, here and now. We are all recycled from the building blocks that have been on Earth since its formation. The assemblage that makes up you, here and now, is unique. You have never existed before and you won't exist again. You also have unique problems that are yours to solve; trust in and be thankful for your ability to do so, even if you can't see the solution today. Give thanks that you exist in this time and place, and for all that you are able to accomplish in this world (even if it feels like things are not going well at the moment). We, just like every other being that exists, are miracles. Be grateful for you.

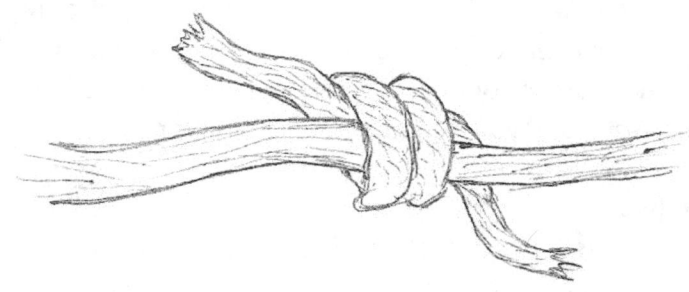

Acknowledgements

I'd like to begin by thanking Kim Frerichs and Denise Foster Scott, who provided steadfast support and encouragement as I worked through the process of bringing this book to life.

I also want to thank my proofreading team for improving the story with their feedback - Amanda Krauss Nguyen, Micah Rogers, Dale Combs, Jack Hartt, Terrie Bay Powers, Sam Gahagan, Jody Sanders, Skyler Walker, and my writing buddy, Corrie Lugtenaar. It was so helpful to have extra eyes on this!

And finally, my deepest gratitude to you, for welcoming this little story into your life. Readers make the magic happen. Without you, this book would be nothing but some inky marks on paper. Thank you, thank you, thank you!

About the Author

Julie Tennis is a writer and philosopher who lives in a tiny logging community in Southwest Washington. She uses metaphor and the written word to contemplate nature and the subconscious to gain insights into how we relate to each other and ourselves. The Gratitude Beads is her first book.

www.ingramcontent.com/pod-product-compliance
Lightning Source LLC
Chambersburg PA
CBHW060359130626
46553CB00003B/1305